Essays on life by Thomas Mitchell, Farmer

Vagabond Voices
Glasgow

Published on 19 May 2014 by
Vagabond Voices Publishing Ltd.,
Glasgow,
Scotland.

ISBN: 978-1-908251-28-2

Printed and bound in Poland

Cover design by Mark Mechan

Typeset by Park Productions

For further information on Vagabond Voices, see the website,
www.vagabondvoices.co.uk

Contents

Back cover photo: Thomas Mitchell (centre), his brother-in-law Tam Finnie (far left), his daughter Margaret Michell (left), and his son William Mitchell (Right). The photo was taken in the early thirties.

Back flap photo: Thomas Mitchell with his wife Margaret and his granddaughters Dorothy and Margaret, taken early forties.

Inside back cover: from left to right, Thomas Mitchell, his sisters-in-law Jean and Mabel (at the back), his wife Margaret and his daughter Margaret in front of her, and a cousin from Aberdeen possibly called Mary. The photo was taken in 1929 or 1930.

Essays on life by Thomas Mitchell, Farmer

Introduction

Thomas Mitchell's world was a more formal one than ours. Formality is primarily about compartmentalisation, so when he sat down to write, he entered a very different mindset from the one he experienced in his working life – and, of course, one very different from our own. It belonged to the last years before the outbreak of a devastating war whose imminence no one could be entirely sure of and whose devastation would then have been unthinkable.

I am not referring here to the clearer distinction between the written and the spoken word, which was very much there of course, but to the many layers of the barrier that divided his everyday life and the talks he gave to the Mutual Improvement Association of Newburgh in rural Aberdeenshire. The language of the essays is Standard English, but the spoken language would have been Mid Northern Scots, also known now as Doric, and the switch in languages would have been mirrored in the change of subject matter and the more solemn trappings. He travelled the four miles from Mill of Ardo to Newburgh by bicycle, one of the inventions that permitted a greater exchange of ideas and experiences at the time. He dressed in his suit and before his appointment with the lectern he would practise his timing and delivery in an empty barn. The Mutual Improvement Association would have been a society of peers, and part of a self-help tradition, but this was still a formal gathering for a serious purpose.

In reading this book, we are being introduced only to one particular Thomas Mitchell, and we have very little information on the other Thomas Mitchells. He was a tenant farmer, and his family had been working the farm at Mill of Ardo since 1791 and would continue to do so until 2002, when his son William died (the farm having been bought by the family in 1959). We know from the family that he was a devout man, but these essays are not a devotional work. Indeed, his essays express a strong belief in self-help and free will – very far from Calvin's predestination.[1] Regular church attendance would have been the norm in rural Scotland at the time – and indeed until a few decades ago. We cannot know if he was also pious, as he keeps religion at arm's length in his writing. Where he does mention it, it is in passing and suggests that he assumes the reader or listener to be similar religious views. The methodology, however, is that of reasoned argument.

Before the First World War, tenant farmers paid

---

1 Mitchell writes, "The colours of the outside world for us depend upon the colours of our own mind. We get in it what we seek or, in other words, the world is to us pretty much what we make it." – "The Art of Living", p. 18.

their rent annually on the same day at the big house, where they were photographed as a group. Having paid his rent to the factor, Mitchell was then paid back some money with which to pay for the laird's drink, in accordance with some local custom, but one year when he found the landowner in a state of inebriation, he decided that more drink was not advisable and returned the money to the factor. Readers of these essays will not be surprised by this restrained and commonsensical behaviour.

Born in 1870, Mitchell was a quiet, hardworking man of regular habits, who married late in life, some years after completing this collection of essays. He may have been a witty man, but you won't find that here. Learning still had something of the sacred about it. We know from the letters of famous writers of the past that it was common practice to keep one's sense of humour well hidden in "serious" works. In other words, very little of the nature of Thomas Mitchell transpires from this text. We may imagine him as a rather severe man steeped in the Scottish Presbyterian tradition, but the few photos we have suggest something more varied and complex (photos too can be misleading).

Where the text and the little biographical information we have meet is on the relationship between work and education, which is a recurring theme. He frequented courses in 1889, 1894 and 1895 on the Principles of Agricultural Science run by the County Council of Aberdeen, and in his pre-war essays he wrote, "The real value of knowledge consists not in the abundance of knowledge that a man may possess, but in the useful purpose to which that knowledge is devoted."[2] "Again, self-culture by the labour, patience and perseverance which it entails, enlarges the individual intelligence, corrects the temper, and forms manners and habits of thought – all of which render one a more useful and efficient worker in the sphere in which his lot has been cast."[3] However he contradicts this pragmatic interpretation of education in the later essays, and provides a more cultural and liberating interpretation of what it is.

Mitchell kept a study in his small farmhouse and his reading was fairly eclectic, although there appears to be a preponderance of the English seventeenth century and the American nineteenth century. The Americans are not only writers but also role models. They are usually Republican and "radical", and everyone was an abolitionist, with the exception of Lincoln who reluctantly passed abolition into law. It was Lincoln who appointed Elihu Burritt to the post of American consul in Birmingham. No doubt Mitchell identified closely with Burritt, who was known as the "learned blacksmith". In times of economic hardship, the polyglot Burritt would return to his trade as a blacksmith. His prominence in some of the great international social movements of the nineteenth century was remarkable.

Mitchell, like everyone else, was an individual, and we cannot take him as a spokesman for social attitudes in rural Aberdeenshire at the turn of the

---

2 "The Secret of Success", p.29.
3 "Education and Its Value", p. 73.

twentieth century. If his studies had taken him in the direction of particular American authors and lives, which he identified with for whatever reason, then he would not presumably be a typical Aberdeenshire farmer.

There's certainly something recognisably American about Mitchell's philosophy: his belief that the free market (not a term he ever uses, because he simply does not see beyond it or perceive the social problems it creates) rewards hard work and benefits both the person who works and society at large. But as we shall see, there is much else besides.

It may be that he was importing American ideas, but it is perhaps even more likely that the ethos of Scottish presbyterianism, a cousin of English puritanism, shared ideological roots with the American non-conformist tradition, which over there was the establishment or close to it. Interestingly, that tradition has all but disappeared in Scotland, while it has become utterly dominant in America (which once had a significant left-wing movement – now lost in historical amnesia).

We have to be very careful, because one of the most striking aspects of this book on my first reading was the emphasis Thomas Mitchell puts on society. He would have found quite alien Thatcher's assertion that "there's no such thing as society." From the very first paragraph in the book, he makes clear that life is a balance of self-interest and duty to society, which has perhaps the greatest call. One quote of the many should suffice: "In the discharge of our daily work we ought to realise that we are not only labouring for our own profit and those who may be dependent upon us, but for the commonweal."[4]

Collectively the essays are a panegyric for work, and this is the most obsessive theme. Work is the great teacher,[5] and work is essential to human dignity. One essay is called quite simply, "The Value of Work", but this argument is not restricted to that essay. "Work thus done," he writes, "becomes the law of our being, … It is the root and spring of all that we call progress, …"[6] "Industry becomes a passport to success. Everybody respects it. Even the lazy man is compelled to acknowledge its value."[7]

As Mitchell's world is one of unremitting hard work and admirable application, it is understandable that he felt this way, especially as he probably chose to be a farmer out of familial duty and not inclination. However, not all the people he admires in this book were as hardworking as he undoubtedly was (though most were and were clearly chosen for that reason). We have to object that many great ideas are the product of a leisured existence or even an idle mind, as is some of the best art and literature.

He asks us to rediscover gentleness and manners: "A kind word in season may be spoken. A word of praise, where praise is deserved. We are all very sparing of praise, but there is more danger of hurting another by withholding it than of injuring him

---

4 "The Art of Living", p. 16.
5 "Work is the best of all educators, for it forces men into contact with others and with things as they really are." – "The Value of Work", p. 45.
6 "The Art of Living", p. 17.
7 "The Secret of Success", p. 37.

by bestowing it."[8] But in amongst the moderation, gentleness and conservatism with a little "c" (I suspect that he voted Liberal), he suddenly reveals a more classist tone: "An artisan who has the essential, unmistakable mark of nature's gentleman, who has no fever for wealth but makes a good use of whatsoever he has, and is himself the evidence that a man's life consists not in the abundance of the things he possesses, who does his work and does it well, a noble, honest artificer and therefore a blessing to his world, who has a kingdom in himself in the cultivation of tastes that ally him to all things lovely and of good report, such a man, with a genuine royalty stamped on him, connecting his best self with all that is best and noblest – a reader, a thinker, a real brotherly man – is quite as convincing an evidence of what education can do, as the millionaire with his riches, or the grand with his grandeur."[9] It is worth quoting this passage in full, because nowhere else does the author write with such passion and rhetoric. A sentence of 138 words is used to describe the ideal man as he perceives him – a man like Elihu Burritt or perhaps Thomas Mitchell himself. This is a man who is not constrained by his manual labour and is proud of this station.

I use the word "station" advisedly, not because it is used by the author, though it is used once, but because he believes in a natural hierarchy, albeit one in which each station has equal dignity. He insists that the rich have a duty to use their wealth for the

8   "The Art of Living", p.21.
9   "Education and Its Value", p. 78.

betterment of society: "A life that is not useful in some way and does not help others in some fashion is a wasted life." Carnegie would express a similar thought: "A millionaire who dies a millionaire is a man who has wasted his life." Equally a man, however poor, "be his habitation the humblest hut", is capable of elevating himself through education and aspiring to the same dignities as everyone else. Within this balanced hierarchy there are cycles driven mainly by the lack of work and struggle in the lives of the rich: "the young man who imagines success an easy thing and begins life where his rich father left off, usually ends up where his father began."[10]

It is in this context of hierarchy that divine providence makes its one brief appearance. "Though all cannot gain distinction, this I do say, that every honest, frugal and hard-working man can make his way, that every man and every woman, under the varying circumstances and conditions which divine providence hath endowed upon them, may and in fact can always make the very most of themselves only if they will."[11] Here providence gets a mention and is then sent packing by free will.

Also in the context of hierarchy, Mitchell advises friendships amongst people of "equal station", as all other friendships are going to suffer from toadying or condescension. He does not comment on whether hierarchy is good or bad, but he suggests that we have to work within it and accept it. This view had of course been challenged for some time, in both

10 "The Secret of Success", pp. 31.
11 "The Secret of Success", p. 29.

the countryside and the industrial cities, but it and Mitchell's considerable optimism and faith in progress were about to be shattered. "It is a beautiful world in which we live," he writes, "and into most lives more happiness than sorrow enters, and most lives might have more happiness in them than they really have, if they sought for it."[12] I doubt that Thomas Mitchell would have repeated that assertion five years later following the conflagration that divides not only the author from us, but presumably also from his older self. He left no written records of how his ideas developed in the aftermath of war, as no doubt they did. The voice in this book is an individual voice but also one of a particular moment. Today, at least in Anglo-Saxon countries, there are attempts to rewrite the history of the Great War once again, and depict it as a just war and an unavoidable cost. This operation is not only unwise, it is impossible: the statistics are insane and must have appeared so even to the generals who gave the orders. If Europeans had bothered to notice the American Civil War, they might have avoided their own one. Railways could move troops about easily and, just as important, could supply them with provisions and munitions. Machine guns could cut down thousands of soldiers before they could make the enemy lines. Exploding shells, fetid trenches and static lines added to the misery. This was a war like no other.

Thomas Mitchell's voice reaches from beyond that obstacle, from a time in which many terrible things occurred and many lived in hopeless slums,

---

12   "The Art of Living", pp. 18.

but in many parts of society it was still possible to believe in human progress and civilisation. Reading this book we become aware of how much we have lost – above all his belief in the integrity of society, which was, I think, a pleasant delusion. There are, of course, aspects of his thought that we are glad to be free of, such as the concept of the undeserving poor, the Taylorist concept of the need to maximise productivity, and a belief in redistribution through charity rather than the state, although these ideas are either returning or becoming even more ingrained in our societies. Taylorism had barely started to count, and so he could not have known how it would affect human relationships in ways he certainly would not have approved of. He rarely mentions women, and in the one case that he does this most clearly, they are defined a little coyly as the "fair sex". In his mid forties, he is critical of the younger generation, as so many middle-aged men have been over the centuries.

Yet his is a strong and characterful voice, and it is one of hope, determination and acceptance. There is also tolerance and moderation. Although there are inconsistencies in this book, one point on which Mitchell is absolutely solid is the primacy of morality, and it relates to self-control, another central theme for this member of a mutual improvement association: "A good conscience is to [a man of self-control] more valuable than any success. He is not so bent on the accomplishment of any plan as to take a dishonourable step to fulfil it. He can have patience. He can bear disappointments. He can yield to insurmountable obstacles, and by gentle and moderate progress is more likely to succeed in the end than others by violence and impulsiveness." There is much wisdom in that. And with the benefit of hindsight, we can see how a few of the things he believed in undermined this central tenet of his thought. We too probably hold beliefs that, unbeknown to us, are undermining values we hold dear. History is made of such uncertainties.

Allan Cameron, Glasgow, April 2014

The Art of Living

The subject which I have chosen for my paper tonight is a very wide one.[1] While choosing it, the question which I wish to ask and in some way to give an answer, is – "How or in what way is a man to make the most of his life, not only for his own comfort, happiness and wellbeing, and that of those who may be dependent upon him, but also for the good, the prosperity and welfare of the community in which he lives."

I cannot enumerate on all the elements which enter the art of noble living, for it is the art of noble living which I wish to treat, but I shall mention three of these elements which seem to me to be the most important.

The first of these is **usefulness**. We are all sent into this world for a purpose: to be useful in some way or other, and to occupy our time in some sort of service not only as a means of gaining a livelihood for ourselves, if we have to work for a livelihood, but also to contribute in some form or other to the good and the welfare of our fellow men.

---

1 Read to the Mutual Improvement Association of Newburgh on 6 March 1912.

Those who are sometimes spoken of as the idle rich and are free from the necessity of work should not spend their time and means in seeking merely their own pleasure. They ought to find a means of being useful in the way of providing work for others, or of spending the large store of the world's riches which have fallen to them, so as to make others, less blessed in this way, happier and better.

A life that is not useful in some way and does not help others in some fashion, is a wasted life.

Every man ought to have the desire to be useful and to seek some form of usefulness; some occupation or work in which he may use his powers and talents in the service of his fellowmen.

To the majority of men their daily work is their main means of usefulness. It may be their only means. The nature of a man's daily work may not be of his own choosing, since circumstances and not choice frequently determine a man's work for him. But whatever nature his work is, whether chosen by his own free will or forced upon him by circumstances, a man ought to perform it to the best of his ability, with a view to making himself useful. Work thus done develops man's nature, stimulates and elevates man's whole being, and cannot fail in many ways to become serviceable to others.

In the discharge of our daily work we ought to realise that we are not only labouring for our own profit and those who may be dependent upon us, but for the commonweal. The farmer, for example, should realise that he does not grow crops and rear cattle merely to pay his rent and keep himself, but that the fruits of his labours are contributing towards the food supply of the nation.

The sailor on his voyages from country to country should feel, in undergoing the hardships and dangers of his calling, that, in addition to securing his means of livelihood, he is bringing merchandise from shore to shore to feed the homes and carry on the industries of different countries. This spirit of usefulness carried into daily work lends a dignity to work and imparts to it pleasure.

Work thus done becomes the law of our being; the living principle which carries men upward and onward. It is the root and spring of all that we call progress, for what is at the root of every invention? What is its first impulse? The desire for some new thing that will be useful, that will economize time, labour and money. All progress and civilisation itself is built upon the desire for usefulness.

Every generation enters upon the labours of the generations that have gone before. It inherits the accumulations and products of its ancestors. Their treasures of skill, art, invention and intellectual culture have all arisen from the desire for usefulness; from the desire of lifting mankind up to a higher and better social and moral condition.

The humblest toiler should therefore feel that, in the discharge of his daily duties to the best of his ability, he is doing something. He may be only contributing an atom, but it is still something – his part in the world's onward march of progress.

I have spoken of those who are under no necessity of work, as we usually understand that word; of those who are independent and have much wealth at their disposal. They do not escape the duty of being useful – of putting their riches in some way to the service of their fellowmen. There are various ways in which they may do this – for where there is a will, there is a way. They may provide work for others or help in so doing, or, they may seek out some form and means of dispensing charity to the needy. They may make themselves useful in these and other ways.

The amount of good done by charity can never be estimated. But that charity may be productive of evil as well as good is a fact that cannot be questioned. Unless money is wisely distributed in charity, it will frequently do more harm than good. There are many forms of benevolence which create the very evils they are intended to cure. They encourage the habit of indolence or foster the spirit of dependence on the part of the unworthy.

True philanthropy consists of endeavouring to relieve misery, suffering and destitution, and seeking to help in time of need those who are willing and anxious to help themselves.

The second element in the art of living is **happiness**, or the search for happiness. Man was made for happiness. It is a beautiful world in which we live, and into most lives more happiness than sorrow enters, and most lives might have more happiness in them than they really have if they sought for it.

One of the best secrets of a happy life is the art of extracting comfort and sweetness from every circumstance. There is a fable about a cold fire brand and a burning lamp starting out one day to see what they could find. The fire brand came back and wrote in its journal that the whole world was very dark. It could not find a place where ever it went in which there was light, everywhere was darkness.

The lamp when it came back wrote in its journal, "Where ever I went there was light". The lamp carried light with it and when it went abroad it gave light to everything. The dead fire brand carried no light and it found none where ever it went.

This is a fable, but it expresses exactly how different people go through the world and what they find in it. Some find light and happiness where ever they go, because they look for it and have the desire in them to find it. Others find little or no happiness anywhere, because they do not look for it, or there is no expectation of it in their own hearts.

The colours of the outside world for us depend upon the colours of our own minds. We get in it what we seek, or, in other words, the world is to us pretty much what we make it. There are many ills and hardships in every life which make the heart at times sore and weary, and the spirit sad, but these do not always last. What is very severe does not last long. If we put a stout heart to a stey brae, they very often disappear, but even when they last, it is not all darkness and gloom. There is a good deal for us to rejoice in even while they last, as the saying is, "there never was a bad, but there might have been a worse".

People are always looking for happiness at some

future time and in some new thing, or some new set of circumstances, in possession of which they some day expect to find themselves. But the fact is, if happiness is not found now, where we are, and as we are, there is little chance of it ever being found. There is a great deal more happiness around us day by day than we have the sense or the power to seek and find.

If we are to cultivate the art of living, we should cultivate the art of extracting sweetness and comfort out of everything, as the bee goes from flower to flower in search of honey.

Happiness does not lie in the mere possession of money, as many think. Money may procure many comforts and pleasures for a man, but it never will, of itself, bring true happiness, for along with the comforts and pleasures it may bring care and worry and an ever increasing and never satisfied desire for more, as we see in the case of the wretched miser. Misused money may be a source of unhappiness.

Happiness depends not on things without us, but on the heart within.

While money cannot bring us happiness, there are many things that can do so. The pursuit of some hobby, reading, reflection or culture may do so. Occupation in anything for which we have a taste or liking, is a source of true happiness to us, and if we would be happy, we must find some such means as these for occupying our leisure time.

Under this heading of the Art of Living, comes the desire of making other people happy. There are many means open to us for doing this. We need not dwell upon material help, that may be given to them in times of need. This is a means that suggests itself to all and is the first to suggest itself. But, it is a means which is within the reach of most of us to a very limited extent. I would mention other means, which do not so readily suggest themselves, which are within the power of each of us and which may be bearers of greater happiness to others than even help of a material kind would be.

A kind word in season may be spoken. A word of praise, where praise is deserved. We are all very sparing of praise, but there is more danger of hurting another by withholding it, than of injuring him by bestowing it. A word of encouragement in times of failure and disappointment; a word of hope to one who is in the depths of darkness or despair; a merry smile, a jocular remark, even a clasp of the hand, go a long way in cheering the heart or lightening the burden of others at seasons when they are in need of sympathy and cheer. They are helped and strengthened much in this way.

If the happiness of others is not thus considered and studied, care should be exercised lest their unhappiness be caused by lack of tact or even rudeness. There are people who, unintentionally, speak the wrong word or give pain when they wish to give pleasure. They are always making allusions to things on which no word should be spoken. They are ever touching sensitive spots. They are continually hurting the feelings of their friends and leaving frowns and tears behind them, for much unhappiness in this world is caused by rudeness. We need only say of it that in every shape and form it deserves the strongest condemnation, for it is the violation of all politeness and good manners.

To seek our own happiness and the happiness of others in the manner described, and to avoid, in so far as we can, causing others unhappiness by wounding their feelings by act or word, I consider to be the second requisite in the Art of Living.

The third requisite of noble living is **character**. The word character signifies a distinctive mark, made by cutting, stamping or engraving, as on a stone, metal or other hard material. That is the meaning of the word by its derivation.

Applied to a person, it signifies the distinctive qualities by which one person is known from another, which give him his personality and make him a person by himself. These qualities may indicate strength or weakness, energy or indolence, goodness or badness, and so we speak of the character as being, strong or weak, energetic or indolent, good or bad.

Character is the result or the effect produced by various things. The first thing that influences it and gives it form is inherited. We receive from nature a certain disposition or temperament. We do not inherit character, but a tendency in disposition and temperament towards a certain character, good or bad, energetic, indolent, rough or gentle, and that original inherited tendency gives a bias towards a special character.

Then there are the surroundings of infancy and childhood, and the company in which life, especially the early years of life, are spent.

Again there is habit, that yielding to or resisting the forces of external influence, which in some way or other are constantly being brought to bear upon us, a process which goes on within us, unconsciously, and which, in course of time, acquires that power over us which we call habit.

All these things go to form character. To give a person his personality, to make him what he is, to make him different from every other person in the world.

In speaking of character as the third requisite in the art of noble living, I mean more than that. To live nobly, a man must have a character moulded by sobriety, honesty, purity, justice and truth. I mean that, but I mean more than that too. I mean he must have decision of character, that he should not be like the weather cock turned about by every wind that blows, changing his opinions and his attitudes or actions in accordance with the opinions and the influences of others whom he may meet from time to time. He should think for himself and speak for himself, realising his personality and his responsibility for everything he does as a man by himself. He should also have moral courage: the courage to stand up for his convictions, and to take what he considers the right and proper course independent of the favour or displeasure of others, and no matter what others may do or say. While adopting this attitude, he ought, at the same time, to be tolerant of the opinions of others who may chance to differ from him. But when his mind is made up, after due consideration and meditation upon any certain thing or certain course of action, he ought to have the moral courage to say and do what appears to him to be the right and proper thing.

Then there is the principle of self-control. Self-control should regulate the whole range of our living, our wishes, our pursuits, our pleasures and our passions. There is, assuredly, nothing unlawful in our wishing to be freed from whatever is disagreeable to our lot and to obtain a fuller enjoyment of the comforts of life, but when these wishes are not tempered by reason or regulated by self-control, they are in danger of drawing us into much extravagance and folly. The desires and wishes are the first springs of action, and when they become inordinate, the whole character is likely to be tainted. In our pursuits and aims – whatever these may be – there is a need for the exercise of self-control, the self-control that will not allow transgression of the bounds of moral duty. The man of self-control, as he is temperate in his wishes, so in his pursuits and aims, is regulated by virtue. A good conscience is to him more valuable than any success. He is not so bent on the accomplishment of any plan as to take a dishonourable step to fulfil it. He can have patience. He can bear disappointments. He can yield to insurmountable obstacles, and by gentle and moderate progress is more likely to succeed in the end than others by violence and impulsiveness.

In regard to pleasure, there is a wide field for the exercise of self-control. By the very law of our being, every pleasure which is pursued to excess becomes harmful – a poison to us. No sooner is the line drawn by temperance and moderation passed, than evil effects come forward and show themselves. Pleasures are an essential of life. If moderately indulged in, they contribute towards health, cheerfulness and vigour, but when no self-control is exercised in regard to them, and anyone gives full rein to them, they may produce ill health, misery and weakness, in body or in mind, or they incapacitate the person in some way from the discharge of his daily work to the full measure of his ability.

And over our passions there is great need for self-control, because there is no passion in human nature which has not of itself, a tendency to run into excess. All passion implies a violent emotion of mind. I would specify only anger and resentment, where the excess is so obviously dangerous, as to call loudly for self-control. He who gives himself up to the impetuosity of such passions without restraint is universally condemned by the world and hardly considered a man of sound mind. Moments of passion are always moments of delusion, for nothing truly is what it then seems to be. All the opinions which are then formed are erroneous, and all the judgements that are passed are extravagant. On no occasion is strength of mind shown by violence of passion. This is not the strength of men, but the impulsiveness and impetuosity of children. True strength of mind is shown in governing and resisting passion, not in giving it scope or in acting, on the most trying occasions, according to the dictates of conscience and temperate reason.

The last element of character which I would mention as entering into the art of noble living is **self-respect**. This term explains itself. It is regard for self. It is not conceit, nor self-love, nor selfishness, but a regard for one's own good name and reputation. It is the constant desire to avoid the contempt or ridicule of others, by outward appearance, company or conduct, and it is the habitual endeavour to shun anything and everything, mean or unworthy, which would make one ashamed of oneself.

No matter how poor or humble a person may be, he may have and should have self-respect. Though I mentioned it last, it is a starting point, the foundation stone of a noble and worthy character. A person who has self-respect will not go very far wrong. If he is found on a wrong path, it is without his knowledge that he is there, and as soon as he finds out his mistake, or has it pointed out to him, he will quit it. Whereas, the person who lacks self-respect is ready for entering any company, following any course of action, and sinking to the lowest depths of degradation. He has parted company with the last and best restraint from evil, and his best friend in the way of help towards what is good and noble and true.

Ladies and gentlemen, my subject may seem to you to be an ambitious one on my part. I know it is a subject whose full and just treatment lies far beyond my thoughts and opinions. I did not know its vast comprehensiveness until I began to prepare my paper, but it is a subject which appeals to me and interests me, as it ought to interest us all, and if it exercises your thoughts and draws forth your observations on it tonight, I shall have gained all I seek. My presentation of the subject for your consideration will be a source of profit to you, as the preparation of my paper has been to myself.

The Secret of Success

What is Success?[1] It is not merely to gratify personal ambition, to accumulate wealth, to win the highest office or to become famous for learning eloquence. One or all of these objects may be acquired and still life becomes a substantial failure.

The highest success is achieved by making the most of one's powers and opportunities. A man with five talents and small opportunities may improve them, so as to be of more real value to mankind than the one with ten talents in the midst of great advantages. The former is more successful than the latter in accomplishing the controlling purpose of life; he has made the most of himself.

The secret of success proper consists in the development and proper use of those faculties which God has given us. Man, therefore, must become his own artificer. He must do for himself what no other person can do for him. The absolute necessity then of intelligence to success is obvious. Every young man should cultivate the mind to acquire knowledge as an element of power, for it is the mind that controls and

---

1 Read to the Mutual Improvement Association of Newburgh on 27 January 1909.

directs. Improve the mind, make it stronger, nobler and a man himself is improved.

It is the birthright of every man to think for himself, to act on his own initiative, and to exercise his powers of observation, as an end toward success. It is quite common-place to say, "Knowledge is power", and generally speaking, knowledge is an element of power, but it does not necessarily follow that knowledge always becomes an element of success.

The real value of knowledge consists, not in the abundance of knowledge that a man may possess, but in the useful purpose to which that knowledge is devoted. It is then, and only then, that knowledge does become an element of success. Most certainly a little knowledge is a very good thing, but at the same time, my friends, remember that a little knowledge after all is many, many times a most dangerous thing.

Now there is not only success, but there are various degrees of success. There is the highest rung of the ladder and there is the next to it. True it is to say that everybody has not the same faculty or power and, therefore, cannot attain the same degree of success compared with that of others. A man may shine in the second rank, who would be eclipsed in the first, so a man may fail in one occupation and succeed in another. He may become a successful merchant and yet fail as an artist.

Though all cannot gain distinction, this I do say that every honest, frugal and hard-working man can make his way, that every man and every woman, under the varying circumstances and conditions which divine providence hath endowed upon them, may and in fact can always make the very most of themselves only if they will. For there is success in every useful occupation for man who will pay its price, but he who wants it for less, is simply half a man.

Then again, there is what is known as a genius, which means to most men great mental powers, or a wealth of natural endowment.

That there are born merchants, philosophers and inventors, where success appears to be their birthright, cannot be denied. However, such elements are only inherited by a few.

The art of seizing opportunities and turning even accidents into account, bending them to some useful purpose, is a great success. The art of discrimination is one of the qualities which eminent men possess in common and hence it should be classed with the elements of success. It is not so much a gift perhaps, as it is a thing of culture.

There is an idea amongst some people and a well nigh fatal one it is, that success in life is an easy thing. As a matter of fact, it is just the very opposite. For remember, the battle of life in the greater number of cases must necessarily be fought uphill and to win it without a struggle is perhaps to win it without honour – for if there were no difficulties, there would be no success. If there were nothing to struggle for, there would be nothing to be achieved. Very few, if any, fully realise the difficulties, trials in every life and, therefore, it is only by patience, perseverance and self-sacrifice, together with an indomitable determination of purpose that these difficulties can be overcome. It is the expectation of difficulties and obstacles, the willingness to begin in a small way, to advance slowly and to bend all the energies to the controlling purposes of life to win the prize, that is the characteristic of a nobleman, the characteristic of a business man and the characteristic of a success-ful man. But the young man who imagines success an easy thing and begins life where his rich father left off, usually ends where his father began. There need no man tell me success in life is an easy thing.

Again there is a popular notion with some who call success simply luck, "Lucky hit", "Lucky fellow". They mean, evidently, that the successful man hap-pened to become rich, learned or great, without fore-thought, plan or purpose – that there was no real cause for his success, and that it was not of his own well directed and persevering efforts. "Lucky man," they say. Now such an idea is well nigh impossible, because it is only by patience and perseverance, together with a well directed and indomitable deter-mination of effort to overcome, that success can be attained. If it were otherwise, why should not luck make a man wise or learned as well as rich? Why should not a man, by mere chance, happen to be a renowned philosopher or a great statesman, or a famous general? Is it more difficult or strange for luck to make a Newton, a Webster or a Wellington, than to make a Gladstone? Such questions then expose the folly of those who believe in luck. I say it is a delusion. Of course, I admit there are some people who have better luck than others do. That there may be, perhaps sometimes is, a grain or element of luck in success after all cannot be questioned.

The business man, for instance, who by luck received from some kind benefactor, either capital or personal influence, perhaps both, which may be the means of introducing him into a larger sphere of business and ensuring earlier success than might otherwise be the case. To the efficient, enterprising young man, who always makes the most of himself, such personal influence then becomes a god-send. But to the easy going, the aimless, the careless, the indifferent class, such capital and personal influence simply becomes useless. Indeed, it is worse than useless.

Now ladies and gentlemen, the question comes to be, "How, or in what way, is this success most likely to be attained?"

The question may naturally appeal to you, "How is it that one man succeeds and why is it another fails?"

It would be superfluous for me to give all the reasons as to the real cause of success or failure, since success or failure, in any sphere of life in the world, may be due to one or other of a few things, or to one or other of many things. I will just mention a few of the essential conditions that are necessary for the fulfilment of a successful life, although they may be as numerous as the sand on the seashore.

My first element of success then is **tact**. Now tact is just the ability to use one's natural powers, acquisitions and opportunities to the best advantage. Under its sway a single talent accomplishes more than five or ten talents without it. Tact then becomes one of the most essential elements of success.

Tact is not a single faculty, but a combination of

faculties. Its existence implies the possession of other powers, as well as this discriminating knowledge of the conditions under which they perform their parts in the drama of life. Just as in this connection we sometimes find that one man will see more with one eye than some do with both.

A simple illustration of tact may be found in the biography of George Stephenson, the renowned engineer, which tells us there were many highly educated engineers in his day, who knew more than he did in all the sciences, but, there were none so apt in applying what they knew to practical purposes as he. Tact then enabled him to reduce his conception to practice. Such then was the secret of his success.

Talent is power. Tact is skill. Talent knows what to do. Tact knows how to do it.

It was said that one of Napoleon's generals understood military science better than he did, but how to use it in the battle-field baffled his powers. The real value of tact then becomes apparent. To possess knowledge, wealth or power without knowing how to use it is next to possessing none of them. What men call shrewdness and common sense signifies tact. Tact enables us to do the right thing at the right time. It adapts us to circumstances and makes us equal to the occasion. Some people say this virtue is more of a gift than culture is. At any rate, if a person be not naturally endowed with this faculty of tact, then that person may develop and improve this faculty by cultivating the habits of close observation.

It was genuine tact in a smaller way, in everyday

affairs, that led Gerrit Smith[2] to settle a dispute between two of his labourers about the milking of a cow, by seizing the pail and milking the cow himself.

The second element of success is **decision and energy**. Now decision is just determination, unwavering firmness. Energy is internal or inherent power and vigour. Earnestness is ardour or zeal in the pursuit of anything.

Courage is that quality of mind which enables men to encounter dangers and difficulties with firmness, boldness and resolution.

All these qualities are related to each other at one point, in that each means what the other means. It is difficult to tell where the one ends and the other begins. These qualities always become an element of power.

In the various spheres of everyday life, the necessity for this spirit of mastery is absolute in every pursuit, and, on frequent occasions, its special use is demanded. Young men must experience rebuffs and encounter serious obstacles in everyday life. None are exempt from hardships and disappointments incidental to life and work. Decision is their faithful ally, if called in the hour of need. Difficulties may prove too much for the man of moderate degree of resolution that often possesses the heart, but decision and energy can save the man from ignominious surrender.

The third element is **perseverance**. The power of perseverance is one of the very finest qualities that

2 Gerrit Smith: American social reformer and staunch abolitionist; one of the Secret Six who financed John Brown's raid on Harper's Ferry.

any person can possess. For the chain of success or failure in any sphere of life in the world, hangs to a very great extent upon this one link, perseverance.

Now perseverance in itself is just persistence in anything undertaken. Scripture represents it as patient continuance. Perseverance is so very closely related to that of decision and energy that I find it a very difficult thing indeed for me to define, where one begins and the other ends.

Perseverance many times steps in to complete the work of decision and energy.

The ship's crew rose in rebellion when Columbus was searching for the New World, because there was no appearance of land, but Columbus prevailed on them to sail for three days longer, and before that time had expired, they hailed the New World. Decision and energy had done well up to that moment, over-coming difficulties. Perseverance then came to the rescue, saved the efforts of decision and energy from failure.

To master the humblest profession, one requires time, patience and persistent effort. It was by perseverance that Abraham Lincoln, born as he was in a log cabin, rose by his own exertions and carved his name upon the highest tablet of fame.

It was by perseverance that James A. Garfield,[3] who was born in the woods of Ohio, ultimately raised himself to be President of the United States.

It was by perseverance that Elihu Burritt, the

---

3   James Abram Garfield (1831-81): twentieth president of the United States and one of the four assassinated presidents; a republican politician and abolitionist.

blacksmith, who learned the fifty languages, became what he was.[4]

It is only by patience, perseverance and persistent effort, that self-culture can be attained.

To educate oneself, is to cultivate and enlarge the mind. Improve it, make it stronger, nobler and greater, and the man, himself, is improved and acquires knowledge as an element of power and ultimately renders himself more apt, skilled and effective in every respect. Perseverance then almost becomes a requirement of success. In every life, you must do it to obtain success. There is an adage which says,

> Let us then be up and doing
> with a heart for any fate,
> still achieving, still pursuing,
> learn to labour and to wait.

Would that many a young man of today valued this quality more fully than he does.

Before passing from this point, I must say that along with perseverance, for success in any line of life, there must be, hand in hand, a certain fitness or adaptability for that particular bent in life.

The fourth element is **industry**. When decision, energy and perseverance possess the soul, industry

---

4 Elihu Burritt (1810-1879): blacksmith and polyglot, he was appointed American consul to Birmingham for a period. He organised the second International Peace Congress held in Brussels in 1848. He was active on a number of social issues, including anti-slavery and the Great Famine in Ireland.

becomes inevitable. It is one of God's conditions for physical strength and long life.

Industry becomes a virtue, in that it produces an inspiring, uplifting, stimulating effect over all the other faculties of the mind. It seems to rally them with all the inherent power they possess for action.

Industry becomes a passport to success. Everybody respects it. Even the lazy man is compelled to acknowledge its value. To be industrious is a bargain every young man must make with himself, for it is not only a necessity, but becomes a duty.

Labour is honourable and it is even more so when taken in the right spirit. Let us remember there is nothing derogatory in any employment which ministers to the wellbeing of the human race. It is the spirit that is carried into an employment that either elevates it or degrades it.

We read that the industrious man shall stand before kings. That the hand of the diligent maketh rich.

The industrious man whose work is honest, well directed, and whose principles have been governed and controlled all through by patience, perseverance, indomitable courage, and by moral principle, according to his opportunities and industry, has made the very most of himself. Also, he who has been inspired, both by the precept and example of others, not only tries to do well, but always tries to do a little better. Such a man never fails to command the respect of his fellow men. Almighty God only helps those who help themselves.

Ladies and gentlemen, in order that you may appreciate more fully the real value of this most excellent virtue, industry, let us look for a little at the baneful effects of its opposite.

Honest work always becomes the parent of wealth. Idleness is the key to beggary. It is the root of all evil.

Work is the law of our being and the living principle that carried men and nations forward.

Industry strengthens, disciplines, elevates, man's whole being. The physical, mental and moral faculties of the body are increased by it, whereas idleness degrades a man, the mental and moral faculties are impaired and they become dormant if they do not altogether disappear. The man himself ultimately almost becomes a thoroughbred loafer.

Industry yields more substantial happiness than idleness.

On the contrary, idleness is the parent of vice and crime. Spurgeon tells us, "The devil tempts all other men, but idleness tempts the devil."[5] Idleness of the mind is much worse that that of the body, for an idle brain becomes the Devil's workshop. Well-earned industry makes many friends, not so with idleness.

Kind assistance to the industrious is a godsend, but help to the lazy always encourages laziness. Help a lazy man and he becomes lazier than he was before. Laziness is always a very loathsome disease. A premium on laziness is sometimes offered by mistake. Experience proves that tramps increase by generous assistance. Give a square meal to one tramp fraternity and you will very soon have

---

5 Charles Spurgeon (1834-92): English Baptist preacher well-known in the nineteenth century. This quote appears to be a Turkish proverb, but Spurgeon did write, "Idle people tempt the devil to tempt them."

a dozen more at your very door before the week is out. They have prodigious memories and never forget where the best food is obtained. All lazy men bear kinship to tramps. The laziest man we ever heard of was in the state prison, New Hampshire. He chopped off one of his thumbs and afterwards attempted to cut off one of his arms, in order to avoid the drudgery of work.

The fifth element is the **Economic Use of Time and Money**. To the money-maker, time is money. To the young man who sincerely strives to make the most of himself, time is more than money. It is culture, character and usefulness.

The waste of time may prove the waste of what is too precious for money to buy. The waste of enterprise and energies, without which neither money nor self-culture can be won, and indeed of mere fragments of time may be to throw away the chances of success. It is here that economy of time becomes a duty.

A faithful improvement of leisure hours alone will accomplish what it has accomplished again and again – excellence in art, science, literature and trade. Now leisure is time for doing something useful. This leisure, the diligent man will obtain, but the lazy man never, for a life of leisure and a life of laziness are two things opposite. Many eminent examples could be given of the economical use of time and some of them show that leisure hours have wrought better results to them than full time has done to others.

It has been said of a European cathedral that when

the architect came to insert the stained glass windows, he found to his great disappointment that he was one window short. At length an apprentice in the manufactory where the windows were made came forward and said that he thought he could make a window that would harmonise with the others and produce the desired effect, from the bits of glass cast aside. He successfully collected the fragments and studied them and finally produced a window that was conceded to be the most beautiful of all. In like manner, we sometimes find that men who have reached the highest attainments and built up the most substantial and comely characters, have done so from the bits of time that have been broken from the edges of a busy life.

Once more, economy of money is not less important than economy of time. A penny saved is as good as a penny earned. Wealth depends chiefly on two words, industry and frugality, i.e. waste neither time nor money, but make the best use of both.

The use of money is the only advantage there is in having money. It is always recognised as a good principle to make money. At least, if wise economy and Christian principle control the method of money making, it is an important duty. Saving is certainly a duty, and every man ought so to contrive to live within his means. This practice is the very essence of honesty, for if a man does not manage honestly to live within his own means, he must necessarily be living dishonestly upon other people's means. Those careless about personal expenditure and who merely consider their own gratification, without regard to the comfort of others, generally find out the real use of money when it is too late.

It is a recognised fact that carelessness and neglect with regard to the real value of this excellent virtue – economy – is one of the chief reasons of so many failures. Many young men set up business for themselves in a dashing way, living in style and keeping up appearances for the sake of an impression. Their gains are equal to their highest expectations. Unfortunately, their domestic arrangements are graduated upon a similar scale.

The stylish man, by recklessness and extravagant living, ultimately involves himself in financial difficulties.

The man who exhibits a spirit of indifference towards being careful about little things, a disregard for small profits and is only content with heaps of gains, is, I say, just the sort of man who is going to fail, and who many, many times, does fail, then runs away and commits some shocking crime in order to extricate himself.

All sorts and sizes of excuses are being continually set up in the extenuation of these failures. They are continually blaming their circumstances for their condition, but they are always very unwilling to blame their condition for their circumstances. They even try to make other people believe what they do not believe themselves. What is twenty times worse still is that they try to make other people believe what they themselves never intend to believe. It is many times more difficult for a man in debt to be truthful, for he often promises to pay when he cannot. Promises make debts and debts make promises. Promises sometimes even ride on debt's back. Promising is one thing, aye, and performing is quite another, for out of nothing, comes nothing.

Economy then, is not only a necessity, but becomes a duty and it is always an element of success.

The last and by no means least element of success is **character**. Character is a subject which is about as long as it is broad and very far reaching. So much so that I feel almost unable to treat it. In fact it might be set aside as a subject by itself.

Character is one of the most essential conditions necessary for the fulfilment of a successful life. It is an element of success which is indispensable, may I say, the one thing – needful.

Character is just the man himself. It is not what a man pretends to be, but what a man really is and which makes him to be the man that he is. It is man that makes the character. It is character that makes the man, for what is the man, but the character. Character is a power which everybody recognises or ought to recognise as the highest and the best. Surely they are few, if any there be, who question or deny its value.

Character is what a man really is, whereas reputation is only what is thought of him. Character is the product of laws. Reputation is sometimes like a man's shadow. It is sometimes shorter and sometimes longer than himself. Knowledge is power and character is power, but character is the greater power, because, unless knowledge is exercised it can wield no power in the world. Whereas character, whether consciously or unconsciously manifested, is always a power.

Good manners, courteous behaviour, form an important part of character and are the manifestations of solid and enduring qualities within.

Good principles carry a man upward and onward, and inspire him with higher motives of life, which bring to him, not only success, but the highest degree of success.

Let me say in conclusion that there is no middle course in life. A man is either getting a little better, if not, he is getting a degree worse. The further up the hill a man goes, he always becomes a better man. The further down the hill a man goes, he always becomes a degree worse. In point of fact, when you see a man going up the hill, almost everybody runs to that man. On the contrary, when you see a man going down the hill, almost everybody shuns him. I repeat, there is no middle stage in life.

> We are building every day
> in a good or evil way
> and the structure as it grows
> will our inmost self disclose
>
> Build it well, whate'er you do
> build it straight, strong and true
> build it clean, and high, and broad
> build it for the eye of God

The conclusion of the whole matter is simply this. It is the incumbent duty of every successful man or otherwise, to qualify himself, for himself, both for the life which now is, and for the life which is yet to come.

The Value of Work

It is a matter of fact that to thoroughly and heartily enjoy life, we must have plenty of work to occupy our time.[1]

Those persons who idle away their time with little or no occupation are surely a burden to themselves and, often at times, to their fellow creatures also.

Work is the best of all educators, for it forces men into contact with others and with things as they really are.

It has been found that the worthiest of all men have been the most industrious in their callings, the most sedulous in their investigations, and the most heroic in their undertakings. Indeed, to work of hand and brain, the world is mainly indebted for its intelligence, its learning, its advancement and its civilisation. In substance and in fact, work is the very law of our being and living principle which carries men and nations forward.

The greatest of men have risen to distinction by unwearied industry and patient application. They may have had inborn genius. Their natures may

---

1   Read to the Mutual Improvement Association of Newburgh on 9 February 1910

45

have been quick, but they had to submit themselves to persevering labour.

Labour is indeed the price set upon everything which is valuable. In fact, nothing can be had without work, except poverty and misery.

Now work is a duty which rests upon every man. It is a law of life, and, in its deepest meaning, it is the service of God and of man, and from that there is no reprieve. Most men must work in order to live, and it is also true that he must work in order to live well. A useful and profitable occupation, diligently pursued, is necessary for a wholesome and happy life. It is, indeed, the great civilising agency, for the necessity to work for daily bread is the root from which all advancement has sprung. Without this necessity there would be no progress, but a constant retrogression to the position of the mere animal.

We are driven on to progress and advancement by our human needs and the desire to gratify them. Work is a duty we owe to the Creator. It is evident from the very powers and facilities with which He has endowed man, that man was designed for work in some shape or form, but he has also a duty in the same way to perform to his fellowmen.

The very existence of society lays upon its members obligations towards one another, and the necessity of giving, as well as of receiving, benefits them. If this idea of benefitting others and enriching the world in some way by our work could be carried into the daily performance of duty, it would give work, in our eyes, a new meaning and make life seem more worth living.

To many, work is regarded just as a means of gaining a livelihood, which is a poor and low view to take of work, for work is something higher and more dignified than that. It tends to the enrichment of our nature, and the development of our character. We are, by nature, just the raw material out of which true men are made. We have to undergo the process of being made something higher and better than we are by nature. We have to submit to the discipline that fashions us to higher ends, and our daily work is the appointed instrument for this purpose.

This is the view of work which I intend to set before you, and I would say then, that we must accept work not merely for the sake of what we can get from it, in the shape of material benefits or this world's good things, and of giving these to others, when we have got them, but also, and first of all, that we may become, by means of our work, all that it is capable of making us.

To attain any great end, men willingly submit to the discipline designed to achieve it. So in their daily work, men should willingly subject themselves to a discipline which is to calculate its higher ends, mental and moral, and what it is capable of producing. If they apply themselves to their daily work in this spirit, then it will raise their whole life to a higher level.

The discipline of daily work breeds in us habits of self-restraint, patience, faithfulness, obedience to law and a well-ordered life.

The true reward of working is not the material

wage it earns in money, position or fame, but in the increased and facile power of working.

The fruits of labour can only be reaped by steady, well directed, faithful labour and the fruits of work are capacities for better work. Work, earnest and methodical, is necessary for success all along the line. Even great mental gifts are rendered comparatively useless, unless applied to definite tasks. No amount of pains, it is true, will accomplish the highest creative work of genius, but many a genius has failed to accomplish anything, to make the mark he might have done, simply because he never submitted to discipline of work.

It is a matter of common observation that the successful man is not always the man with the most ability and most brilliant powers. But every true great man has, in addition to his splendid gifts of mind, the additional gift of industry.

Practical industry, wisely and vigorously applied, produces its due effects. It carries a man onward, brings out his individuality and stimulates the actions of others. It also has its fruits of character. Its richest gains are here, not in any outward success, but in the results which work out in the man himself, in giving him the habit of application and discipline of thought, and stiffening his power of will.

In all labour, there is profit, though it cannot be put down in terms of cash. Every youth should be made to feel that his happiness and well-being in life must depend mainly on himself and the exercise of his own energies, rather than upon the help and patronage of others, for labour may indeed be a very hard master, but generally it is found to be the best taskmaster.

It is regarded as the main root and spring of all that we call progress in individuals, nations and civilisation. It has its difficulties, but the school of difficulty is the best school of moral discipline, for nations as for individuals. Wherever there is difficulty, the individual man must come for better or for worse. Much will be done if we but try. Nobody knows what he can do till he has tried, and few try their best till they have been forced to do it.

No great and single work can be accomplished without a long training in the best methods of working. I do not mean that any methods can be a substitute for the original gift, but I do mean that even the greatest gifts need the discipline and development of hard work. Simplicity and ease are the marks of all great work. So simple and easy such work may seem that one is inclined to think that any one could do it. So it seems, but so it is not in reality. It is the product of the one and not of the many. Simple and easy as it seems, there are, behind it, years of toil and arduous learning. It is often these things, and only these, which enable one man to do with ease what others cannot do at all.

The determination to realise an object is the moral conviction that we can and will accomplish it. Our wits are sharpened by our necessity and the individual man stands forth to meet and overcome the difficulties which stand in his way.

Well now, it is struggling against difficulties that our best faculties are brought into play, because it evokes strength, perseverance and energy of character. Thus, our antagonist ultimately becomes our best help.

The school of necessity has often been the mother of invention, and the most prolific school of all has been the school of difficulty. The most ordinary occupations will furnish a man with opportunities or suggestions for improvement, if he be but prompt to seize them.

We are many times compelled by our necessities to adapt ourselves to our circumstances and to take full advantage of our opportunities. Nevertheless, it is not ease but effort and not facility but difficulty that make men. Those difficulties are however our best instructors, as our mistakes very often form our best experience. We very often find out what will do, just by finding out what will not do. No true and lasting work can be acquired except by patience and perseverance.

Perseverance is one of the essential elements of success in every kind of work. Perseverance in itself is just determination and unwavering firmness. Perseverance is energy made habitual, and perseverance in labour, judiciously and continuously applied, becomes genius.

Genius may be somewhat difficult to define. To most men it may mean great mental powers, and that is so, but when analysed, we find it to be intense energy along some line. In fact, the very capacity to labour intently and intensely is of itself in the nature of genius.

The great difference between men consists, less

in their original endowment, than in their power of continuous and persevering labour. There must, however, be the spark of creative power, otherwise, labour, by itself, could avail little.

Men of genius are, for the most part, enthusiasts. In all cases, strenuous individual application is the price paid for distinction in work, excellence of any sort being invariably placed beyond the reach of indolence. The very greatest of men have been among the least believers in the power of genius. The extraordinary results effected by dint of sheer industry and perseverance have led many distinguished men to doubt whether the gift of genius be so exceptional an endowment as it is usually supposed to be. It must nevertheless be sufficiently obvious that without the original endowment of heart and brain, no amount of labour, however well applied, will produce a Shakespeare, a Byron or a Burns.

Numberless instances of men could be cited in this and other countries, who by dint of persevering application and energy have raised themselves from the humblest ranks of industry to eminent positions of usefulness, both in society and in the state.

It was by work that James A. Garfield, born in the woods of Ohio, raised himself to be President of the United States. It was by work that Sir Richard Arkwright gathered together the scattered threads of ingenuity, which already existed, and invented the spinning cotton machine. It was work that enabled James Watt to become the inventor of the steam engine, for after ten years of patient, persevering efforts, he ultimately achieved the sure result of a long continual application. It was hard work that enabled Elihu Burritt, the blacksmith, to master sixty languages. It was work that enabled George Stephenson, the renowned engineer, to become the practical man that he was.

Numberless other instances could be cited of men who have worked their way up from obscurity and poverty to positions of eminence and wealth through difficulties and hardships by their own persistent efforts, making the best improvement of their time and abilities.

On the contrary, there are those who fail. Numberless cases could be cited of those who do fail, but nobody cares very much to hear about failures. Nobody wishes very much to hear about generals who lost their battles, engineers who blew up their engines, architects who only design deformities, painters who never get beyond daubs and merchants who scarcely ever keep out of the Gazette.[2]

It is true that the best of men fail in the best of causes. But why? Even these men did not try to fail. No, nor even regard their failure as meritorious. On the contrary, they tried to succeed and looked upon their failure as a misfortune. Failure in any good cause is honourable, whilst success in any bad cause is infamous.

At the same time, success in the good cause is unquestionably better than failure. Even if a man

---

2 *The Edinburgh Gazette* is the official organ of the United Kingdom government in Scotland and it publishes notices of insolvency and bankruptcy cases.

does fail in his best efforts, it will be a satisfaction to him to enjoy the consciousness of having done his best.

Excellence in all the various spheres of work can only be accomplished by the dint of painstaking labour. It is never granted to a man, but as the reward of his labour, and those resolved to excel, must submit to a continuous application of their powers. Excellence is the result of a continuous application to work of the most carefully disciplined skill, skill that comes by experience in the best methods of working. The cultivation of this quality is of the greatest importance, resolute determination in the pursuits of all worthy objects being the foundation of great work.

Now, it is energy that enables a man to force his way through irksome drudgery and dry details, and carries him upward and onward in every work. It is not eminent talent that is required to ensure excellence in any pursuit, so much as purpose, not merely the power to achieve, but the will to labour, energetically and perseveringly. Nothing that is really worth having can be achieved without courageous working.

A man owes his growth chiefly to that striving of the will that encounters difficulties and which we call effort. It is astonishing to find how often results apparently impracticable can thus be made practicable. An intense anticipation itself transforms possibility into reality – our desires often being but the precursors of things which we are capable of performing.

If you have great talents, industry will improve them, and if you have but moderate abilities, industry will supply their deficiency. Labour is still, and ever will be, the inevitable price set upon everything which is valuable and we must be satisfied to work with a purpose and wait the result with patience. All progress of the best kind is slow, but to him who works faithfully and hopefully and zealously, the reward will doubtless be vouchsafed in good time. Nothing is denied to well-directed labour, and nothing is to be obtained without it.

Daily experience shows that it is energetic individualism which produces the most powerful effects upon the life and action of others, and really constitutes the best practical education. Schools, colleges and academies give but the merest beginning of culture. The culture thus given must be supplemented. Its supplement is the life education of daily work given in our homes, in the streets, behind counters, in workshops, at the plough and in the busy haunts of men. This is the finishing instruction, as members of society, which Schiller designated "The Education of the Human Race", consisting in action, conduct, self-culture, self-control, i.e. all that tends to discipline a man truly and fit him for the proper performance of the duties and business of daily life. A kind of education this, but not to be learned from books or acquired by any amount of mere literary training.

All experience serves to illustrate and enforce the lesson that a man perfects himself by work, more than reading. Work educates the body as study educates the mind. Training of young men in the use of tools would, at the same time that it educates them in common things, teach them the use of their hands and arms, familiarise them with healthy work, exercise their faculties upon things tangible and actual, give them some practical acquaintance with mechanics, impart to them the ability of being useful and implant in them the habit of persevering effort. Heaven helps those who help themselves, is a well tried maxim.

The spirit of self-help is the root of all genuine growth in the individual, and exhibited in the lives of many. It constitutes the true source of national vigour and strength. National progress is the sum of individual industry, energy and uprightness, as national decay is of individual idleness, selfishness and vice. The government of a nation is usually found to be but the reflex of the individuals composing it. The nation itself is only an aggregate of individual conditions, and civilisation itself is but a question of personal improvement of the men, women and children of whom society is composed. The function of a government is negative and restrictive rather than positive and active, being responsible, principally, for protection of life, liberty and property.

Laws wisely administered will secure men in the enjoyment of the fruits of their labour, whether of body or of mind, at a comparatively small personal sacrifice. But no laws, however stringent, can make the idle industrious, the thriftless provident, or the drunken sober. Such reforms can only be effected by means of individual action, economy and self-denial, better habits rather than by greater rights. Indeed, all experience serves to prove that the worth and strength of a state depends far less upon the form of its institutions, than upon the character of its men. If this view be correct, then its follows that the highest patriotism and philanthropy consists not so much in altering laws and modifying institutions, as in helping and stimulating men to elevate and improve themselves by their own free, independent, and individual action.

What we are accustomed to decry as great social evils will, for the most part, be found to be but the outgrowth of man's own perverted life, and though we may endeavour to cut them down and extirpate them by means of law, they will only spring up again with fresh luxuriance in some other form, unless the conditions of personal life and character are radically improved.

It may be of comparatively little consequence how a man is governed without, whilst everything depends upon how he governs himself within. The greatest slave is not he who is ruled by a despot, but he who is in the thrall of his own ignorance, selfishness and vice. Nations who are thus enslaved at heart cannot be freed by any mere change of masters or institutions, so long as the fatal delusion prevails that liberty solely depends upon and consists in government. The solid foundation of liberty must rest upon the individual character, which is also the only sure guarantee for social security and national progress.

Old fallacies as to human progress are occasionally turning up. Some call for Caesars, others for nationalities, others for acts of parliament. This doctrine shortly means, "Everything for the people, and nothing by the people". A far healthier doctrine to inculcate among the nations, would be that of self-help, which, when exhibited in the energetic action of individuals, furnish the true measure of our power as a nation. All nations have been made what they are by the thinking and working of many generations of men – by patient and persevering labours in all ranks and conditions of life. Cultivators of the soil, explorers of the mines, inventors and discoverers, manufacturers, mechanics, philosophers and politicians, all have contributed towards the one grand result, success in work. One generation building upon another's labours carries them forward to still higher stages.

The living race has thus, in course of nature, become the inheritor of the rich estate provided by the skill and industry of our forefathers, which has been placed in our hands to cultivate and to hand down, not only unimpaired but improved, to our successors. Indeed, we can finish nothing. Others begin where we leave off, and carry on our work to a stage nearer perfection. We have to bequeath to those who come after us a noble design, worthy of imitation. Well done, well doing, and well to do are inseparable conditions that reach through all the ages of eternity.

Thrift

My subject tonight is **thrift**, which means the economical management in regard to money or property. Private economy is another name for it.[1]

The object which prompts thrift is generally the amelioration of our social condition, and that of those dependent upon us or related to us. While that is its primary object, it has an end far more important even than that – an end undreamt of when the thrifty people began to save and to put their small savings to account.

It is thrift that produces civilisation. It is thrift that builds houses. It is thrift that builds ships. It is thrift that digs the mines. It is thrift that opens the workshop and supports the employees. It is thrift that keeps up the store. It is thrift which constitutes a nation's power. Therefore, every thrifty person becomes, to some extent, a public benefactor, and it thus becomes evident that every man is not only justified, but bound in duty as a man and as a citizen, to increase his earnings by all fair and honourable means and to lay some part of them aside.

---

1 Read to the Mutual Improvement Association of Newburgh on 4 February 1914.

Thrift is not a natural instinct. It is an acquired principle of conduct. It is not natural because it involves self-denial, the denial of present enjoyments, and the subordination of animal appetite to reason, forethought and prudence. Though an acquired principle of conduct, it does not require superior knowledge, superior intellect – nor any superhuman virtue. It merely requires common sense and the power of resisting selfish enjoyments. In fact, thrift is merely common sense in every day action, and competence and comfort, which are its fruits, lie within the reach of most people – were they to take the adequate means to secure them.

It is not so much what a man gets, as the manner in which he spends what he gets, that is the important thing. A man who earns thirty shillings a week may really be richer than one who earns so many pounds a week, for he may spend his shillings more carefully and wisely than the other does his pounds, and also have more in his purse at the end of the week than the other has.

When a man obtains by his labour more than enough for his personal and family wants – if he has such additional wants to provide – and lays by a little store of savings besides, he unquestionably possesses the elements of social wellbeing.

When we use the term thrift, our first thoughts bring us to money, but there is a thrift or economy in work in the shape of order and system, as well as in the mere coins of the realm, though, of course, thrift hereto ultimately means and ends in money – for, as in a sense time means money, as does order, system or method in work.

It is wonderful how much work can be got through in a day, if we go by the rule – map out our time, divide it off, and take up one thing regularly after another. To drift through our work, or to rush through it in a helter-skelter fashion, ends in comparatively little being done. "One thing at a time" will always perform a better day's work than doing two or three things at a time. By following this rule, one person will do more in a day than another does in a week – "Marshal thy notions" said old Thomas Fuller, "into a handsome method. One will carry twice as much weight trussed and packed, as when it lies untoward, flapping and hanging about the shoulders".[2]

Fixed rules are the greatest possible help to the worker. They give steadiness to his labour, and enable him to go through it with comparative ease. Many a man would have been saved from ruin if he had appreciated the value of method in his affairs. In the peasant's cottage or the artisan's workshop and in the chemist's laboratory or the shipbuilder's yard, the two primary rules must be: "For everyone his duty" and "For everything its place".

Speaking of order brings our thoughts to the home, for unless there be order and thrift in the home, it matters little how much or how little the wage-earner and the breadwinner brings in, the result is the same.

---

2 Thomas Fuller, *The Holy State and the Profane State* (London: William Pickering, 1840), pp. 141-42. T. Fuller (1608-61): cleric, historian and writer, who supported the royalist cause, but found protection under the Commonwealth and thrived during the Restoration.

This will especially interest the fair sex of our audience, for the organisation of the home depends, for the most part, upon the woman, upon her character, her temper, and her power of organisation. A man may be economical, but unless there be economy at home, his frugality will be comparatively useless. How happy does a man go forth to his work, and how doubly happy does he return from it, when he knows that his means are carefully husbanded and wisely applied by a judicious and well managing wife. That is, perhaps, the truest economy, where there is the best housekeeping and the worthiest domestic management. The home then becomes so pleasant and agreeable that the man feels, when approaching it, that he is about to enter a sanctuary – so that the Bible teaching is found to be true and speaks of "A prudent frugal woman" as being "a crown of glory to her husband".

I have spoken of the object of thrift. Now as to its origin.

Self-respect lies at the foundation of thrift. Self-respect is, in itself, a most important thing. Its very practice is elevating and imparts strength to the character. It produces a well regulated mind, it fosters temperance, it is based on forethought, and it strengthens prudence, the dominating principle of character. It gives virtue the mastery over self-indulgence and, above all, it secures comfort, drives away care, and dispels many vexations and anxieties which might otherwise prey upon us. As I have said, it lies at the foundation of thrift.

"The world," once said Mr Cobden,[3] to the working men of Huddersfield, "has always been divided into two classes, those who have saved and those who have spent, the thrifty and the extravagant. The building of all the houses, the mills, the bridges and the ships, and the accomplishments of all other great works – which have rendered men civilised and happy – have been done by the savers, the thrifty, and those who have wasted their resources have always been their slaves."

Note these words of that great statesman: "Those who are in a position of slaves can have no self-respect." A man with something saved, no matter how little, can boldly look the world in the face. Possessed of a little store of capital, a man walks with a lighter step, and there is always the possible evil or rainy day, and he has the satisfaction of knowing that he is prepared for it.

As men become wise and thoughtful, they generally become frugal. Therefore, a wise man thinks of the future, he prepares in good time for the evil day that may come upon him. Economy then, with this object in mind, is a very important duty.

The spirit of independence also lies at the foundation of thrift. We are often told that the spirit of "Scottish Independence" is dying, that we have not the same spirit of independence that our fathers had. Be that as it may, it goes without gainsay, that there are many nowadays who will accept doles of charity from others, or doles from the State, to relieve

---

3   Richard Cobden (1804-65): manufacturer, politician and keen advocate of free trade.

them in some way from the burden of the upbringing of their family, and who use these doles to no good purpose, in as much as they spend what might thereby be saved from their weekly earnings and laid aside for some necessary use. They spend it on mere unnecessary pleasures or enjoyments. It is difficult to see where the independent spirit of such people is.

A spirit of independence, along with self-respect, instigates the first step of improvement. It stimulates a man to rise to look upward, to develop his intelligence, to improve his condition. It is the root of most of the virtues – chastity, reverence, honesty, sobriety – and the man who improves himself, improves the whole world, because he adds one more true man to the mass – and the mass being made up of the individuals, the result is, the improvement of the whole.

The accumulation of money seems to be the passion of the age – more so than in any of the ages that are past – men are too eager to become rich.

It is not the accumulation of money with a desire to do good with it, to help others, to promote industry, to advance the commonweal, for were that the desire and motive behind it the accumulation of money might be praised and not blamed. But it is the miser's passion, who makes money his God, who hugs it and seems only anxious to see how much he will gather and leave behind him when he dies, or the desire to secure it for his own gratification in luxurious living, to cut a dash and make an appearance in the world, that too frequently lies behind men's undue haste to be rich. With the wrong motive behind it, the accumulation of money becomes, as we have been told by the wise man,[4] the root of all evil, and we see the proof of it day by day, in undue speculation, gambling, betting, swindling or cheating.

We study political economy and let social economy shift for itself. Regard for No. 1 is the prevailing maxim.

To save money for avaricious purposes is altogether different from saving it for economical purposes. The saving may be accomplished in the same manner by wasting nothing and saving everything, but here the comparison ends. The miser's only pleasure is in saving. The prudent economist spends what he can afford for comfort and enjoyment, and saves a surplus for some future time. The avaricious person makes his gold his idol, whereas the thrifty person regards it as a useful instrument, and as a means of promoting his wellbeing. Let every man who can endeavour therefore to economise and save, but not to hoard. Let him nurse his little savings for the sake of promoting the welfare and happiness of himself and others.

I go a step further than saying that accumulation of money seems to be the passion of the age. I say extravagance is the pervading sin of modern society. It is not confined to the rich and moneyed class, but also extends to the middle and working classes. With the rich or well-to-do, outward appearance is considered the great thing, the most desirable thing. It is something grand to be regarded as a somebody, whose

---

4 Saint Paul: the famous quote is from 1 Timothy 6, 10. In the First Epistle to Timothy, it is the "love of money" that is "the root of all evil".

acquaintanceship is worth having and sought after. Appearances must be kept up – they must seem to be rich, live in a certain style, inhabit handsome houses, give good dinners, drink fine wines and have a handsome equipage – all this, perhaps, though it can be accomplished only by overreaching or dishonesty.

Some who cannot go so far, or aim at so high things as others yet go too far along the same line, aim at what they consider as respectability, but they have the wrong idea of what respectability is. Respectability, in its true sense, is a desirable thing. To be respected, on the right grounds, is an object which every man and woman is justified in seeking to attain. But the modern idea of respectability consists of external appearances. It means wearing fine clothes, dwelling in fine houses and living in style. It looks to the outside, to sound, show and externals. It listens to the clink of gold in the pocket.

Moral worth or goodness forms no part of modern respectability. A man in these days may be perfectly respectable in the eyes of the world, and yet be really and truly despicable.

There is nothing wrong in seeking respectability if people seek it by honest and legitimate means. But this is what many will not do. They do not consider the true cost – they deem that it must be secured at any cost. So they attend to their dress, their establishments, their manner of living and their observance of fashion and in spending their money, in a sense, before it is earned, by running into debt at the grocers, the milliners and the butchers. They must entertain their fashionable "friends", at the expense of the shopkeepers, but when misfortune overtakes them and when their debts have been overwhelming, "their friends" prove only "summer friends", for when the evil day comes, as it always comes, in due course, they fly away and shun the people who are up to their ears in debt.

Sir William Temple tells us, "that a restlessness of men's minds to be something that they are not and to have something that they have not, is the root of all immorality."[5] It is not however so much in the fact that mere appearances are kept up, as in the means taken to keep them up, that the fruitful cause of immorality is to be found. The seeming rich man, when he has gone the pace too rapidly, often descends to immorality, rather than to descend in apparent rank and too often yields to dishonesty, rather than sacrifice the mock applause and hollow respect of that big fool "the World".

How often do we see or hear instances of great men and much respected men, who from one extravagance or another, from wantonly squandering wealth, which was not theirs, in order to keep up a worldly reputation and cut a fine figure before their admiring fellows, all ending in a sudden smash, a frightful downfall, an utter bankruptcy – to the ruin, perhaps, of thousands. Vain men will sometimes give up their lives rather than their class notions of respectability. We never hear of a man committing suicide for want of a loaf of bread, but it is often done as a means to escape justice for misdeeds.

---

5 Sir William Temple (1628-99), *Essays* (London: John Sharpe, 1821), vols. 2, Vol. 1, p. 149, in "The Different Conditions of Life and Fortune", pp. 143-54.

To be rich or to have the appearance of riches is esteemed as a merit of a high order, whereas to be poor or to seem so ranks as something like an unpardonable offence. However, it is no disgrace to be poor – the praise of honest poverty has often been sung. Robert Burns tell us:

> What though on hamely fare we dine,
> Wear hoddin grey, and a' that.
> Gie fools their silks, and knaves their wine,
> A Man 's a man for a' that.
> For a' that, and a' that,
> Their tinsel show, and a' that
> The honest man, tho e'er sae poor,
> Is king o' men for a' that.

That man is not poor who can pay his way and save something besides. He who pays cash for all that he purchases, is not poor, but well off.

Poverty has its blessings as well as its privations – nothing sharpens a man's wits like poverty. Poverty often purifies and braces a man's morals and the poor are often the happiest people – their lot in this respect, far excelling the wealthier and the really rich.

Whilst honest poverty is honourable, misery is humiliating, in as much as it is for the most part, the result of misconduct, and no one who has health and strength, if he exercises prudence, temperance and maintains a good character, need be in misery. The working man's lot in this country has improved in many ways within the last quarter of a century – within a shorter period than that – and is still improving. It is his own fault if, granted health and strength, he be otherwise than comfortable and happy.

Comparatively few people can be rich, but most have it in their power to acquire by industry and economy sufficient to meet their necessary wants. It is not the want of opportunity, but the want of will, in the way of economy, that stands in the way of this. Men may labour unceasingly, with hand or head, but if they cannot abstain from spending too freely and living too highly, they will have nothing in the end for all their labour.

Education and Its Value

Education. What does the term signify? It is in everybody's mouth, statesmen, journalists, philanthropists, the man in the arm-chair and the man in the street. Persons of all sorts and conditions are everlastingly discussing matters pertaining to education.

If I put it to you – What do you mean in your use of the word? I dare say you would at once think of schools, colleges and universities, of school boards, of lessons and examiners, and of inspectors of the machinery, which a mysterious department called the Scottish Education Department (perhaps better known as My Lords) sitting at Dover House, Whitehall, controls and the purpose of which is to turn out the youth of the country with a certain amount of knowledge and a capacity to take the place which personal aptitudes or necessities indicate in the struggle for existence in the work of the world. Is not this, you would ask, what is covered by the word "education"?

Well, but in all this, what we are regarding is not the end, but only the means towards the end, not the reality itself, but only the tributaries to it and the conditions that are essential to its possession.

This brings us now to consider more fully the real

nature of education itself. The original root, from which the word is derived, simply means to lead out. Education is the art of leading out, the reference to something within, to powers and capacities that are to be stimulated, led and trained. What is put in is put in with a view to its being called out and so far as this calling out is fulfilled, it becomes a power. In other words, knowledge is power.

The essential question for us is – How to live? Not how to live in the mere material sense only, but in the widest sense. The general problem which comprehends every special problem is the right ruling of conduct in a direction, under all circumstances – in what way to treat the body, in what way to treat the mind, in what way to manage our affairs, in what way to bring up a family, in what way to behave as a citizen, in what way to utilize those sources of happiness which nature supplies, how to use all our faculties to greater advantage, for ourselves and for others – how to live completely? This, being the great thing needful for us to learn, is by consequence the great thing which education has to teach.

Mr. Ruskin tells us, "Education is the leading of human souls to what is best and making the best out of them. You do not educate a man by telling him what he knew not, but by making him what he was not."

If all this is true, and I think no one here will dispute it, then to prepare us for complete living is the function which education has to discharge, and the only rational mode of judging an educational course is to judge in what degree it discharges such a function.

However, education is not for the benefit of the individual alone, but also for that of the community of which he is a member. The good old book tells us that no one liveth to himself and no one dieth to himself. This is true in a material or physical sense as in a spiritual sense. The young should be taught to believe that their life is a gift given them, not only for their own sake, for their own good or benefit, but for the sake of the community in which they live. The powers and faculties within them are, therefore, to be cultivated and called out of them, not for their own sakes only, but for the sake of others.

The life of the individual cannot be completed without training him in the duty that he owes to the community. He is to be brought up in the consciousness that he does not live to himself, that he has got a brain, hands and strength in order that he may do work and live a life that shall be useful, not only to himself, but to the nation as a whole. More than that, while the individual unit is to be perfected, he never can become as an isolated unit. He is a social animal, society his country. Humanity has just claims on him, for he is a complete, true, fully developed person in the measure in which he is a part. An educational course then must bear this fact in mind and make provision for it accordingly.

It ought ever to be borne in mind by school masters and teachers of the youth of every generation that all men and women, young and old, should remember that when school days or college days are over, they are ever their own school masters as to how they live, what they are to be and do in the various spheres of their existence, and in the various aspects of their responsibility.

From the root idea of education as a leading organiser of the forces and properties of our being, the conceptions and aims of educationalists, theoretical and practical have been evolved.

What a vast continent, we may even say universe, the term education covers. It is no less than this, that which is to be fulfilled, shaped out and wrought out in all places, departments, periods and aspects of life.

Now narrowing our view to one point, within the wide range that is included in the term education, we move on to discuss the acquisition of knowledge and mental discipline and how it can be utilised.

The acquisition of knowledge is attained mostly by self-culture. The function of the teacher is to develop and guide the powers and faculties in the plastic time of life. His purpose should be to lead out the pupils' powers, not merely to pump knowledge, as it were, into them, to interest his pupils and to make them partners in the world of education. A teacher ought not to work for, but with his class, and strive in all his methods of instruction not so much to teach directly, as to guide his scholars in their efforts at self-education or self-culture.

The best teachers have been the readiest to recognise the importance of self-culture, by stimulating the students to acquire knowledge by the active exercise of his own faculties, to rely more upon training than telling, to make pupils themselves active parties to the work in which they are engaged. They have thus made teaching a thing far higher than the mere impartations of scraps and details of knowledge. They have made it the impartation of a new spirit to their pupils, the bestowal of a learning desire and the zeal to develop their powers by their own active efforts, rising gradually, step by step, to higher statures, preparing for life's vocations, and by this very process, to evolve all that is best in them, to come as near as possible to a complete living.

Knowledge acquired by self-culture has a double advantage over that which is merely imparted by oral teaching, in that it gives a greater vividness and permanency of impressions. Facts thus acquired become registered in the mind in a way that mere imparted information can never effect.

Again, self-culture by the labour, patience and perseverance which it entails, enlarges the individual intelligence, corrects the temper, and forms manners and habits of thought – all of which render one a more useful and efficient worker in the sphere in which his lot has been cast.

The blessings or fruits which education has brought to man and the world cannot be estimated. What education, in the form of scientific knowledge, has done in the field of human industry alone is impossible to say. The changes which it has brought about in regard to manual labour by the introduction of machinery baffles all description.

Opinions may differ as to the good or evil which these changes have brought about in the way of superseding manual labour by machinery, but there can be no two opinions as to the fact that these changes have multiplied enormously, the amount and the variety of articles of human production on which rest the prosperity and wealth of a nation.

In the age in which we live, there is a commercial rivalry; an ever increasing commercial rivalry between the various nations of the world. Indeed, it has come to this, that the nation which does not pursue scientific knowledge, which does not give to its artisans, its young lads, who are to be the artisans of the future, a scientific education, must fall behind in the race.

For the making of a thorough, intelligent workman, in any practical branch of industry, a comprehensive scientific knowledge is essential. For their own interest, no less than for the prosperity of the nation as a whole, men must think and act with the fullness of intelligence.

The man of the future, be he farm labourer, mechanic or artisan, is not to be a fellow whose luck is up or down with a shilling in his pocket. He is to be a man of knowledge, both theoretical, experimental and practical, who understands all the laws of successful operations. The future is in the hands of those who make the best use of their ability, their opportunity, their time, and the best use, in all the ways, of brain, will and hand.

The value of knowledge to any man depends not on its quantity, but mainly on the application which he can make of it. Often do we find those who have been the most brilliant scholars, who have carried off the highest prizes at school or college, turn out comparative failures in life. It is not the best educated teacher who is always the most successful teacher – very often it is the other way about. It is not always the most learned clergyman who is the best preacher.

Behind knowledge there must be the power to apply it – if it is to be of real profitable value. It is this power of application that many want. Everyone who seeks a livelihood through the portals of what, in ordinary language, we call education should consider not in what direction he would like to apply his education, but in what direction he is fitted to apply it – in other words, in what particular direction his bent lies.

Knowledge of itself does not make a man a better man. It may even make him a worse man. A dishonest man may become a greater scoundrel, through education, than he would have been uneducated. We see instances of this day by day.

But knowledge should make a man a more successful and happier man. It will enable a man to adapt himself more readily to circumstances, suggest improved methods of working and render him more apt, skilled and effective in all respects. It will not enable him to get rid of the daily work of life, but it will sweeten his daily work for him by elevating his conception of his labour, by allying it to noble thoughts which confer a grace upon the lowliest as well as on the highest rank.

No matter how poor or humble a man may be, if he be a cultivated and intelligent man, the greatest thinker may come and sit down with him, and be his companion for the time, be his habitation but the humblest hut, self-culture may exercise the most beneficial influence over the whole tenor of a man's character and conduct. If it does not bring him wealth, it will, at all events, give him the companionship of elevated thoughts.

But what is self-culture? Reading, in itself does not constitute self-culture. It may be culture, in a way, but not self-culture, in the sense in which we usually understand the term. Unfortunately, much of our reading is little short of a sort of intellectual dram drinking, imparting a grateful excitement for the moment, without the slightest effect in improving and enriching the mind. It is unaccompanied by reflection and meditation, and much literature read is really not worth the reading, in as much as it has in it nothing to leave behind and very little to reflect upon. Thus, many indulge themselves in the conceit that they are cultivating their minds when they are only employed in the humble occupation of killing time. Self-culture is reading or study accompanied by reflection and meditation.

To those who have the eyes to see and the mind to reflect, life's experiences may be as good a teacher and even a better teacher than the lifeless page of a book. The experience gathered from books, though often valuable, is but of the nature of learning, whereas the experience gained from actual daily life is of the nature of wisdom. A small store of the latter is worth vastly more than any stock of the former. Useful and instructive though good reading may be, it is only one mode of cultivating the mind and is much less influential than practical experience.

The object of knowledge should be to mature

wisdom and improve character, and render us better, happier, more useful, more benevolent, more energetic, and more efficient in the pursuit of every high purpose in life. We must ourselves be and do, and not rest satisfied merely with reading and meditating over what other men have been and done. The best light must be made life, and the best thought action. At least we ought to be able to say, "I have made as much out of myself as could be made out of the stuff", and no man should require more, for it is every man's duty to discipline and guide himself, with God's help, according to his responsibilities and the faculties with which he has been endowed. The first worth of a man or woman is manhood or womanhood. He or she is something more than a hand. More than all the crafts and craftsmen is the humanity.

The culture to which I give first place is that which gives width to man's horizons, length to his perspectives, richness to his thought, intellectual, artistic and moral fullness and completeness to his life.

The use of education is not to be identified with the idea of getting on, of rising to a higher social place or making more money. Education has a far deeper and far broader meaning than that.

It is quite right for an ingenious youth to aim at betterment of condition, and I cannot blame him if his ambitions soar to high and lofty places. But what I protest against is the tendency to urge the value of education as being a means of "getting on", as it is called.

Now to place that in the front is thereby to encourage the feeling that educational success is to be measured by the quality of the cloth on the back, to the prefix, to the name or to the depth of the purse. We are pointed to this one and that one who began as poor boys and ended as rich men, or famous men, and the comment is, "See what education did." All right, let every facility be given to the lad of good "pairts", but I choose to see what education does in quarters where the chronicler fails to notice it.

An artisan who has the essential, unmistakeable mark of nature's gentleman, who has no fever for wealth, but makes a good use of whatsoever he has, and is himself the evidence that a man's life consists not in the abundance of the things he possesses, who does his work and does it well, a noble, honest artificer and therefore a blessing to his world, who has a kingdom in himself in the cultivation of tastes that ally him to all things lovely and of good report, such a man, with a genuine royalty stamped on him, connecting his best self with all that is best and noblest – a reader, a thinker, a real brotherly man – is quite as convincing an evidence of what education can do, as the millionaire with his riches, or the grand with his grandeur. The fullest value of knowledge is its power of making life – the life that is the real worth of persons and of nations – interesting, giving it zest. It can be an emancipation from the tyranny of circumstances, and from things debasing and deteriorating and can impart a real unfading splendour to the properties of the soul, supplying a meat of which the mind eats and the world knows not.

Is not this the effect, more or less, of a truly liberal education, and education which is within the reach of all of us?

May I say to you, with all your getting, get this: combine in your possessions, wisdom and knowledge, be always adding and preparing for a more complete and ever more complete life. There are difficulties in the way, but it is these difficulties that test and increase the strength.

Friendship

Friendship has been regarded in all ages as one of the most important relationships of life. Cicero says that it is the only thing on the importance of which mankind are agreed. It has been defined by Addison, the great English writer, as "a strong habitual inclination in two persons to promote the good and happiness of each other."[1] It has been termed by another, "the golden thread that ties the hearts of the world."[2]

From what these writers have said of it, it is manifest that friendship is more than a source of pleasure, that it is an inspiration even in the education of life. Friendship is the free spontaneous outflow of the heart, and the joy that comes from true communion of the heart with that of another is perhaps one of the purest and greatest in the world. It is not an end in itself, but rather most of its worth lies in what it leads to, that is the priceless gift of seeing with the

---

1 *The works of Joseph Addison, Complete in Three Volumes Embracing the Whole of the "Spectator" & C.* (New York: Harper and Brothers, 1837), Vol. II, p. 106, issue no. 385. John Addison (1672-1719): English essayist, poet and playwright, and co-founder of the *Spectator*. On this internet, this quote is generally attributed to Eustace Budgell, Addison's slavish imitator who continued to work for the *Spectator* after Addison's death.
2 This quote is from John Evelyn (1620-1705): English writer and diarist.

heart, rather than with the eyes, of learning to love all kinds of nobleness, which give insight into the true significance of things.

With this description of friendship, I would say a few words on the selection of friends. We make connections and acquaintances and call them friends, and the method by which friendships are brought about differ greatly, depending largely on temperament. Some people have a genius for friendship. They are of a genial and likeable disposition, open, sociable, unselfish, and of a responsive nature. Others again are of a more naturally reserved disposition, finding it hard to open their heart even when their instincts prompt them.

In the selection of friends, it would be wise to obtain equality of friendship, that is to say, equality of station, of circumstance. If a man is poor and chooses for a friend one who is rich, the chances are either that he becomes a toady and a mere "hanger-on" or that he is made to feel his inferiority. Young men, in this way, have been led into experiences that they could not afford, into society that did them harm, and into debts sometimes that they could not pay.

Making friends of those beneath us is often equally a mistake. We come to look upon them with patronising affability.

Either to become a toady, hanger-on or a patron is destructive of true friendship. We should be able to meet on the same platform and join hands as brothers, having the same feelings, the same wants, the same aspirations. We should be courteous to the man above us, and civil to the man beneath us, but if we value our independence and manhood we will not try to make a friend of either.

Again we should not make a friend of one who is without reverence for what we deem sacred and have been taught to deem sacred. Friends should be chosen for character, goodness, truth and trustworthiness, and because they have within them the power of inspiring us with an elevating influence. They may, on the other hand, have an opposite effect on us. They may degrade us, hence the importance of the selection of good and true friends.

In the second place then, let us think of the importance of friendship. It is regarded by others as a test of our character, for the worth of a man will always be rated by his companions. The proverbs of all nations show this. "A man is known by the company he keeps." "Like draws like." "Birds of a feather flock together." If our companions are worthless, the verdict of society on us will be that we are worthless also. This verdict may not in all cases be true, but the probability is that it will be. If we are admitted to the friendship of men of honour, integrity and principle, people will come to believe in us. We would not, they will feel, be admitted into that society, unless we were in sympathy with those who compose it. If we wish therefore that a good opinion should be formed regarding us by others, we need to be especially careful as to those with whom we associate closely and whom we admit to intimate friendship.

Again, friends have a special power in moulding our character. It is the common explanation of a young man's ruin, that he had bad companions. We may go into a certain society confident that we will hold our own, and that we can come out of it as we go in, but as a general rule, we find ourselves mistaken.

The man of strongest individuality comes, sooner or later, to be affected by those with whom he is intimate. There is a subtle influence from them, telling upon him, that he cannot resist. He will inevitably be moulded by it. Here also the proverb points to the lesson. "He who goes with the lame," says the Latin proverb, "will begin to limp." The rapidity of moral deterioration in an evil companionship is its most startling feature. It is appalling to see how soon an evil companionship will transform a young man, morally pure, of clean and wholesome life, into an unclean, befouled, trifling good-for-nothing. Lightning scarcely does its work of destruction quicker, or with more purpose.

It is difficult to give precise rules in regard to the formation of friendship. "A man that hath friends," says Solomon, "must show himself friendly." A man of generous and sympathetic disposition will have many friends and will attract to himself companions of his own character.

We will consider some of the essentials of a true, lasting and beneficial friendship. The first requisite then for making a friend is trust. There must be magnanimity and openness of mind before such a friendship can be formed. We must be willing to give ourselves freely and unreservedly, for we can do nothing without a certain amount of trust, and so much more necessary is it in the beginning of a deeper intercourse.

There must also be, in the second place, kindred spirit, witnessed by the same or like hobby, or the cultivation of some commitment, or an object such as we members of the M.I.A. of Newburgh all have. As an instance of kindred spirit binding friends together, we can find none better than that of Jonathan and David given in the Bible.

In the third place, there should be mutual benefits in friendship. The one friend should, in some way or other, be the complement of the other. That is, strong where the other is weak, helpful where the other requires help. One man can give to his friend some quality of sympathy, or some kind of help, or can supply some social need which is lacking in his character or circumstances. Such sympathy and thoughtfulness must be expressed and not only felt, for it is the expression of it that keeps our sentiment in evidence to both parties. If we never show our kind feeling, what guarantee has our friend, or even ourselves, that it exists. As trust is necessary for forming friendship, faithfulness is necessary for keeping it. For the golden rule is, "To do to and for your friend what you would have him to do to and for you is the whole duty of friendship."

Fruits of every special friendship vary according to the character of the friends and the closeness of the binding, but some general fruits and blessings connected with true friendship may be mentioned.

The first is sympathy, for amid all the vicissitudes of life, sorrow and disappointment, men ask for sympathy and ache to let their grief be known and shared by a kindred spirit. To find such is to dispel the loneliness of life and to have a source of relief for our griefs, our doubts and our fears.

Sympathy is, however, more readily given in adversity than in success. In success, it is difficult to give at times, even by a friend, on account of the envious spirit that possesses most men. It is comparatively easy to sympathise with a friend's failure, while we are not so true hearted about his success. When a man is down on his luck, he can be sure of a certain amount of sympathy. It is sometimes difficult to keep a little touch of malice or envy out of congratulations. It is sometimes easier to weep with those who weep, than to rejoice with those who rejoice – not so much with the people above us, but with our equals. When a friend succeeds, there may be a certain fear that he is getting beyond us, passing out of our sphere and perhaps will not need or desire our friendship so much as before. True sympathy does not recognise such grudging sympathy, but rejoices more for the other's success than his own.

A second fruit of friendship is help, for help is obtained from friendship in the formation of judgement upon certain subjects and questions. Most men have a certain natural diffidence in coming to conclusions and forming opinions for themselves – we rarely feel confident until we have secured the agreement of others in whom we trust. We all realise the advantage of taking counsel of a trusted friend in regard to courses of action to be followed from time to time. In talking a subject over with another person, one gets fresh side lights into it, new avenues open up, and the whole question becomes larger and richer. Amid the difficulties and perplexities of life the mutual counsel of friends is a great asset. It gives strength to the character, and sobers and steadies through a sense of responsibility which one friend feels for the other.

When men face the world together and are ready to stand shoulder to shoulder, the sense of comradeship makes them strong. This help may not often be called into play, but to know that it is there, if need be, is a great comfort. Friends do not always flatter but help, when need be, by pointing out weaknesses in one another, and when this is done, it is performed in a kind and loving manner which causes no offence. In all our relations with each other, it is usually more of an advantage if advice comes from friendly encouragement and not mere correction. Criticism is a good thing but does not consist, as so many critics seem to think, in mere deprecation but rather in appreciation and the critic putting himself sympathetically in another's position and trying to look at things from his point of view and seeking to value conscientious and well-meant work. More good work is lost from want of appreciation than from too much of it. The critic's work must be carefully done!

In conclusion, I would say that to live without friends, suspicious of others and careful of our own interests only is to dishonour and hurt our own nature. We cannot live a self-centred life without feeling that we are missing the true glory of life. We were made for social intercourse – the joy which true friendship gives is a proof of it. We sin against ourselves if we let our affections wither, for our hearts demand love as truly as our bodies demand food. Comradeship is one of the finest and strongest forces in life. A mere strong and capable man, however successful, can be even more successful through comradeship. He not only benefits from that comradeship, but also benefits others in turn.

All royalties from this book will go to **Crathie Opportunity Holidays**, a charity based at Crathie, Aberdeenshire, providing self catering holiday cottages designed and equipped to meet the needs of disabled children and adults.

Situated in a beautiful paved courtyard looking over the River Dee towards Balmoral Castle, and in the heart of the Cairngorms National Park, these four cottages offer holiday accommodation to disabled people, many of whom previously had never enjoyed a holiday in the company of their families, friends or carers. Because of the on site staff, equipment and facilities, a new experience is opened up for many who come back year after year.

However all this equipment is expensive to buy and maintain and because the charity sticks to the principle that disabled people should not have to pay any more than abled bodied people for their holidays, fundraising is an ongoing consideration.

Thomas Mitchell, author and farmer would have been delighted that his essays are going some way to help such an excellent project. Thank you for your support.

Crathie Opportunity Holidays,
The Manse Courtyard,
Crathie,
Ballater,
Aberdeenshire,
AB35 5UL

Tel: **013397 42100**

Email: **info@crathieholidays.org.uk**

Web: **www.crathieholidays.org.uk**

Scottish Charity No: SCO27590

Patron: The Duchess of Rothesay